101 Quips and Quotes

... that will strengthen and sweeten your marriage and family relationships

Ada Adeleke-Kelani

WestBow Press books may be ordered through booksellers or by contacting:

WestBow Press
A Division of Thomas Nelson & Zondervan
1663 Liberty Drive
Bloomington, IN 47403
www.westbowpress.com
844.714.3454

Because of the dynamic nature of the Internet, any web addresses or links contained in this book may have changed since publication and may no longer be valid. The views expressed in this work are solely those of the author and do not necessarily reflect the views of the publisher, and the publisher hereby disclaims any responsibility for them.

Any people depicted in stock imagery provided by Getty Images are models, and such images are being used for illustrative purposes only.
Certain stock imagery © Getty Images.

Interior Image Credits:
#21 – Pastor and Mrs Adeleke Kelani
#36 - Pastor and Dr (Mrs.) Obi Almona

ISBN: 978-1-9736-8938-6 (sc)
ISBN: 978-1-9736-8939-3 (e)

Library of Congress Control Number: 2020906205

Print information available on the last page.

WestBow Press rev. date: 11/23/2020

WESTBOW
PRESS®
A DIVISION OF THOMAS NELSON
& ZONDERVAN

Contents

Dedication

This book is dedicated first to God Who blessed me with:
- my one and only husband, 'Leke who I prefer to refer to as "Ademi" and
- our two amazing sons, Obasegun and Ibunkunolu
This book is also dedicated to the three of them.

Acknowledgment

This book would not be possible without my dearest husband and sons who not only encouraged me to write this book but also provided the inspiration for several of the quips and quotes you'll read in the following pages. I am truly blessed among men.

I also want to acknowledge my dear friend, Pastor Dr (Mrs) Chinyere Almona for all her support - reading and rearranging my manuscript. She is one of my friends who inspired and continues to confirm one of my favourite quotes (#76) in my first book. Indeed 'the friends you choose, "choose" your future.' Thank you, Chi!

My appreciation also goes to the rest of my family, starting with my brothers: Chuma and Emeka, their wives: Akunna and Kaweng, and their families – they each have a very special place in my heart, my extended family: the descendants of: the Madus, the Mkparus, the Anyiwos and my families-in-love: the Kelanis, the Ch,olloms and the Ahiwes who in their unique ways continue to help me appreciate marriage and family relationships – and inspired some of the quips and quotes too.

An African proverb goes something like this, "A single broomstick cannot sweep clean. It takes several broomsticks working together to sweep". And that is how I feel about you, my readers. There is little value in writing a book if it is never read by others. Thank you for being part of this success story; it is my hope that this book will make your marriage and family relationships strong and sweet success stories.

In closing, one thing I enjoy giving and receiving regularly in my marriage and from my family members is hugs. Here's my extension of that "gift" to you.

Hugs from here
Ada

Introduction

This year is a very special one for my husband and I – and for our two sons too.

Sunday March 8, 2020 marked exactly 22 years to the day that my now, one and only husband proposed to me. Yes! He proposed on Sunday March 8, 1998. We got married two years later and twenty years later, we have so much to be grateful to God for.

I have seen and learned - from personal and others' experiences - that being married brings out the best and sometimes the worst in one. Marriage and family relationships are both blessings and if you are not careful, familiarity could breed contempt. We each need to be careful, not careless, about our marriage and family relationships and seek ways to strengthen and sweeten them.

Marriages and families are at the core of every stable and successful society. If we get both relationships right, the world will be all-right.

It is my deepest desire that as I have done and plan to continue to do, that you also adopt and adapt these quips and quotes in your marriage and family relationships. Without a doubt, that is one way we can make our world a better one. We're all in this together and all together we can do it!

Section 1: Marriage matters

1. Marriage is a fragile gift from God to us and needs to be handled with care and love.

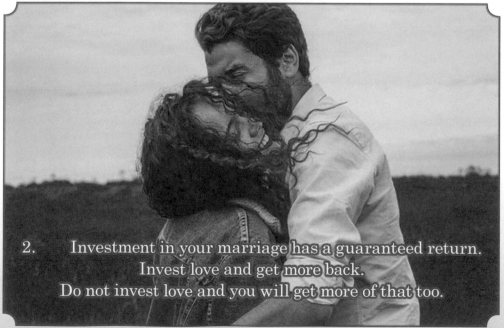

2. Investment in your marriage has a guaranteed return.
Invest love and get more back.
Do not invest love and you will get more of that too.

3.   Love is a partnership...each person needs to be a generous giver and gracious receiver.

LOVE BOAT

4.   Friendship always takes a marriage further than the "love-boat".

5.   Marriage should be based on friendship, so if love fizzles... your friend "ship" will still sail.

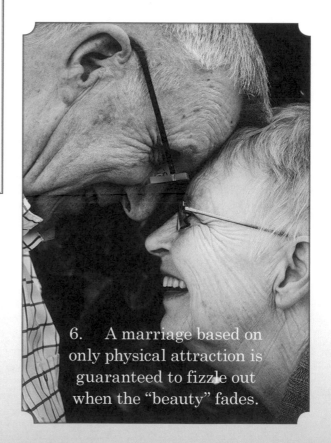

6.   A marriage based on only physical attraction is guaranteed to fizzle out when the "beauty" fades.

7. The best recommended daily intake (RDI) in any marriage is heart-loads of love.

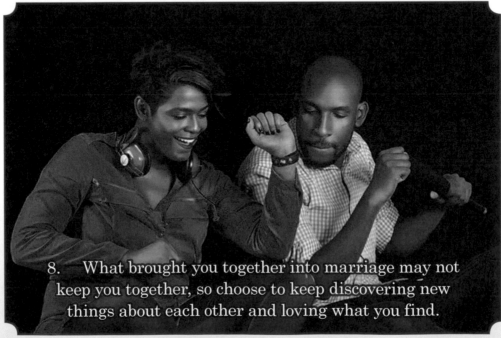

8. What brought you together into marriage may not keep you together, so choose to keep discovering new things about each other and loving what you find.

9. Liking your spouse is very important because you need that when you do not feel like loving him/her.

10. Every marriage is fuller and fulfilling when you have fondness, fun and some funds.

11. We need to love people the way they want to be loved, not the way we want or choose to love them...especially our spouses who we chose ourselves.

12. Do your part to be considerate and appreciate how your spouse chooses to appreciate you.

13. Trying to outdo each other may result in your marriage being undone, if you are not careful.

14. In marriage, you're to complete and complement each other not compete with each other.
It also helps to compliment each other now and again.

15. Complimenting your spouse
complements you
(in ways no one can compete with).

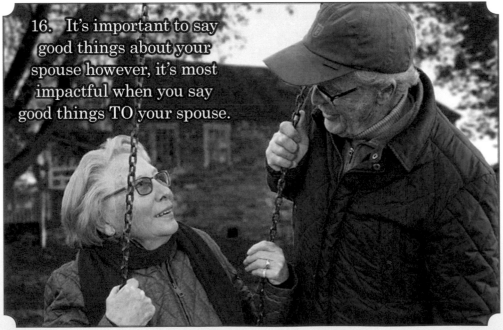

16. It's important to say
good things about your
spouse however, it's most
impactful when you say
good things TO your spouse.

17.   Back up your spouse especially behind their back – they are trusting you not to back-stab them.

18.   If you continually question your spouse's love for you, you may lose what you have.

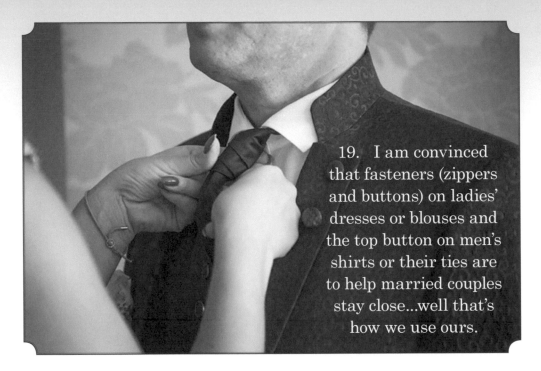

19.   I am convinced that fasteners (zippers and buttons) on ladies' dresses or blouses and the top button on men's shirts or their ties are to help married couples stay close...well that's how we use ours.

20.   Time spent with your spouse is always timely and also timeless.

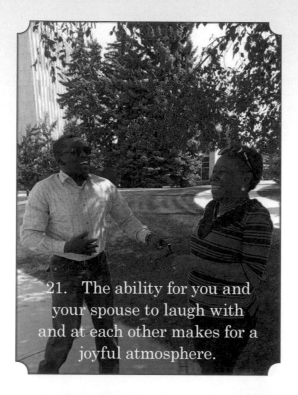

21.   The ability for you and
your spouse to laugh with
and at each other makes for a
joyful atmosphere.

22.   Being two-gether is
a state of heart and mind
not just your hands.

23. Great gains of being together come when you two
gather your resources to make your lives better
– it is not one-sided.

24. Hearts beat as one when you stay together
not when you stray away.

25. The best marriages are lived heart-in-heart
not just hand in hand.

26. When you cherish and nourish your marriage,
it will flourish.

27. Your marriage may not seem as good as another
person's but if you look closely you will see some good in
your marriage.

28. Marriage is about the blending of hopes and dreams
not burying your hopes and dreams.

29. What a blessing when a man knows that his wife is a treasure & does all he can to treasure her.

30. You should boost your spouse's dreams and desires not burst them.

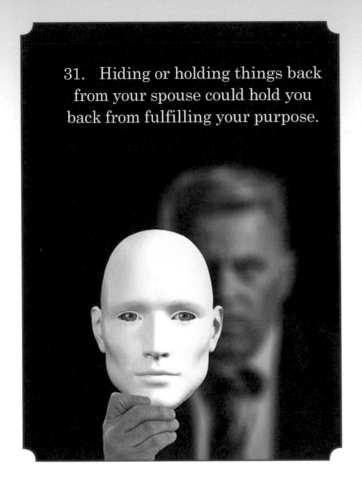

31. Hiding or holding things back from your spouse could hold you back from fulfilling your purpose.

32. Holding your spouse back from pursuing their passion may result in your purpose passing you by.

33. The way you and your spouse handle your
marriage matters matter
otherwise sooner than later,
your marriage will no longer matter.

34. In marriage, you cannot be fully engaged if you are
partially estranged from your spouse.

35. Sometimes, it may seem easier to walk away from your marriage, but you shouldn't because hard work always pays — work on your marriage to enjoy it.

36. Your struggles in marriage should make you snuggle more — because together you can overcome them.

STUDIO 24

37.   Sometimes how you feel does not matter as much as how it will make your spouse, family, friends and others feel if they know how you really feel.

38.   A wise wife knows not to get in-between a man and his mother. And a wise husband knows how not to let his mother get in-between him and his wife.

39.   Your career and/or calling must never come before your care for your spouse and children.

40.   The only third party every marriage needs and must have is God.

41.   Your successful marriage creates a solid foundation for your family.

42.   Wives, any thing with more than one head is a monster... make sure your family does not become a monster. Acknowledge and submit to the God-ordained head of the home – your own husband.

43. Husbands who do not love and "serve" their wives as themselves are doing themselves a disservice.

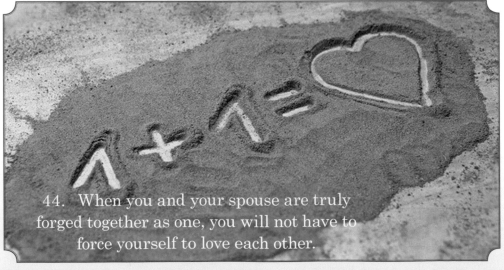

44. When you and your spouse are truly forged together as one, you will not have to force yourself to love each other.

45. Giving each other massages are a medium for passing messages of affection.

46. Sex in marriage should be a "staple"... just never let it get stale.

47. Prioritize your marriage, so it doesn't become a mirage.

48. If you push your spouse and/or children away temporarily, they may decide to stay away permanently.

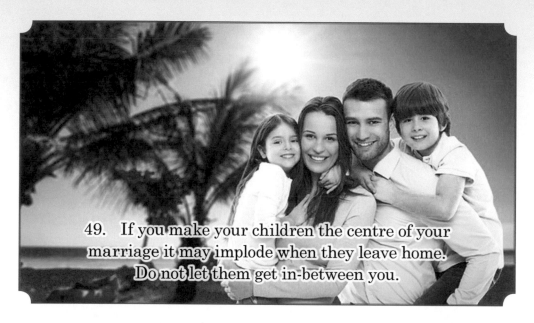

49.   If you make your children the centre of your marriage it may implode when they leave home. Do not let them get in-between you.

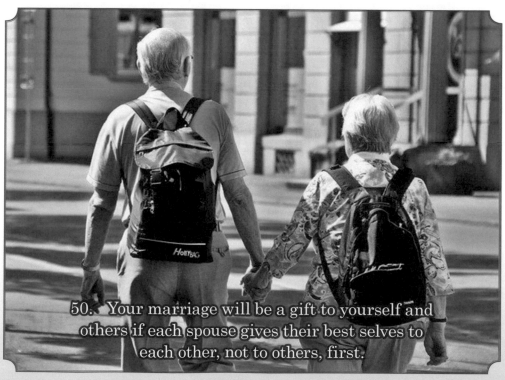

50.   Your marriage will be a gift to yourself and others if each spouse gives their best selves to each other, not to others, first.

Section 2: Family fundamentals

51.   Children cannot choose their parents but can choose who they become based on how their parents raise them.

52.   When it comes to virtues, you can train or drain your children.

53.   Parents, you either correct or corrupt your children by your conduct.

54.   If you pester your children, they may grow up and become unpleasant to be around.

55.   Children are cultured by consistency of character.

56. A parent's influence should be apparent in the life of each child they have.

57. It's only the values you instill in your children that they will leave with and live by when they leave home.

58.   Talking to your children gives you
inroads and insight into their thoughts
so you can guide them along their path
to fulfill their potential.

59.   Parents must never
be too busy to bond with
their children.

60.   When you spend time with your children doing what is important to them, they know that they are important to you.

61.   Working with your children on little things can encourage them to do bigger things.

62.   You can teach your children how to make something out of nothing and how to make more from some small things.

63.   It is easier for children to value and live by the family values their parents value and live by.

64. Parents, without a doubt your children's report cards are important and evidence the quality of their input.

Similarly, your children are your report card and evidence of your input...

What grades will you get on yours?

65. People rate parents based on the children they have raised... not just by those they have praised.

66. Being a parent comes with an awesome responsibility and amazing perks of raising the next generation and being appreciated for it in time.

67. Do what you can to answer your children's questions so that they do not go to the wrong people or places for their answers.

68. When you know, show and go the right way, your children will more likely than not follow your way.

69.   Fathers, your sons learn how to treat their wives from how you treat yours (their mother).

70.   Mothers, your daughters learn how to treat their husbands from how you treat yours (their father).

71.   Childhood is usually the shortest part of a human's life and needs the longest attention.

72. Being a parent is not (just) a call to friendship with your child – it is a call to true love that makes you do what is best for your child at all times.

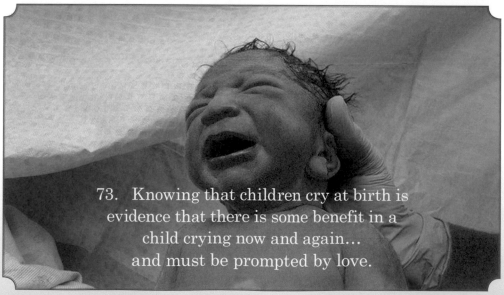

73. Knowing that children cry at birth is evidence that there is some benefit in a child crying now and again... and must be prompted by love.

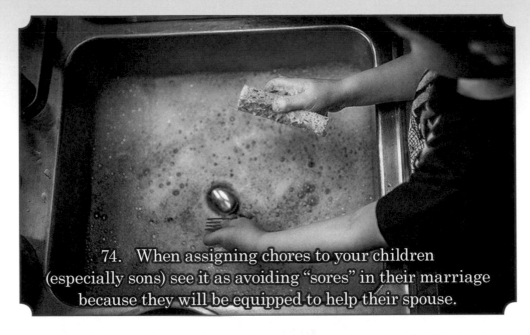

74. When assigning chores to your children (especially sons) see it as avoiding "sores" in their marriage because they will be equipped to help their spouse.

75. Children can learn how to do chores while having fun.

76. Good fathers see and support their children to go farther.

77. Good mothers know how to mold their children without smothering them.

78. Passing on values and virtues from generation to generation requires more than leaving it to genes.

79. Being a grandparent is an opportunity to contribute more to the future as you support them learn new skills.

80. If your children are important to you, it's important that you do not keep important instructional information away from them.

Our Family DREAMS L·A·U·G·H·S WORKS PLAYS & LOVES TOGETHER

81. No matter how friendly you are with your children, they must know that you are their parent not their pet.

82. Children learn from their parents how to progress as they process failure and success.

83. When you make rules and refuse to abide by them, you show your children that rules do not matter.

84. Being too fluid when raising your children could result in them becoming unstable adults.

85. Courtesy, or the lack thereof, is contagious... children are first exposed to it through their parents.

86. The returns, or lack thereof, from our children are directly correlated with our investment in them.

87. Each child is unique and should be **C**losely **H**eld **I**n **L**ove **D**aily.

88. You can never make up for time not spent with one child with time spent with a another (e.g. younger) child.

There are no do-over opportunities because each child is YOUnique.

89. Sibling rivalry does not have to be a reality in your home. It's up to parents to establish the reality they want.

90. Family bonding should be a beautiful benefit not a boring burden.

91. Time spent with your family is
time invested, not wasted,
and the returns are unbeatable.

92. As parents, no matter how tired
you are, you can never retire
and cannot be fired
because you were not hired. ☺

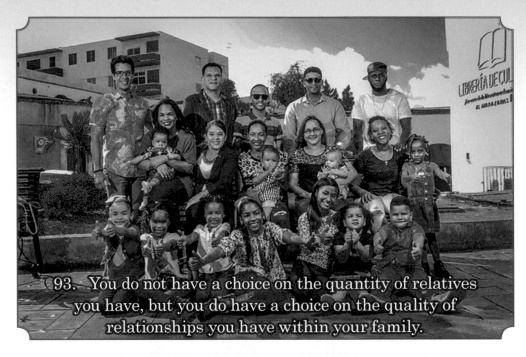

93.   You do not have a choice on the quantity of relatives you have, but you do have a choice on the quality of relationships you have within your family.

94.   Failure to prioritize your family increases the probability of your family being a failure.

95. Bruises heal but memories are
difficult to erase.
Make your children's memories ones
they don't want to erase.

96. The best homes are ruled by the heart
not just by the head and by hands.

97. Children are a gift from God and are good at
regifting the virtues we give them.

98. Your nuclear family should not live in deficit
because of the benefits you extend to your extended family.

99. Live such that you leave a legacy
your children love and live by.

100. Like marriage, parenting is a partnership –
each parent must do their part
if you want to raise a child that is whole.

Last and definitely not least

Here's the quip that completes this book from the one-and-only person God gave to complete me.

101. We are advised not to put all our eggs in one basket. However, in marriage, you must put all your eggs in one basket. – Leke Kelani

Conclusion

This book was inspired my deep desire to celebrate two of the best parts of my life – my marriage and family relationships.

In life, we start from family to marriage to family – then the cycle continues with the next generation. I have learned from experience that what you give or take from your marriage and family will determine if that cycle is a virtuous one or vicious one.

I know that there are so many other quips and quotes out there about marriage and family relationships. It is my hope that the quips and quotes in this book will add to the wealth of wisdom in the world and also strengthen and sweeten your marriage and family relationships.

Other information

Some readers' reviews about:
***101 Quips and Quotes that will charge
and change your life***

"A good read. Words that encourage us to be better and do better; To believe the best for ourselves and others." – Geraldine Egboche

"I received 101 Quips and Quotes as a birthday present and read it immediately. It was well written with lots of wise words and insights for modern day living. I loved the pictorial representations which helped convey and re-enforce the message. I even loved the pink pages. I actually used a pink highlighter pen to highlight the quotes that resonated with me for future reference. An excellent read!" - Teresa

"A most delightful book. If you love good encouraging quotes and would like easy access to the collections, this is the book for you. It is witty, interesting and very inspiring." – Maureen Nwajiaku

"Ada never disappoints. I purchased her book looking forward to feeling the same positive spirit and reading encouraging words that I experienced when I had the pleasure of working with her. She has satisfied that and more with her words of wisdom in the book. Thank you for continuing to share with us and beyond." - Chantal

"Ada's book was like a ray of sunshine and left me inspired and motivated to be the best I could be. I keep my copy on my desk and I refer to it whenever I need a boost of positivity in my life. This book is a multivitamin for your spirit!" – Sylvane Quillien

Autographed copies can be ordered at: https://discoveryourbrilliance.blogspot.com/

Printed in the United States
By Bookmasters